Little

Activity Book

Becky J. Radtke

DOVER PUBLICATIONS, INC.
New York

Bibliographical Note

Little Zoo Activity Book is a new work, first published by Dover Publications, Inc., in 1995.

International Standard Book Number:
0-486-28845-5

Manufactured in the United States of America
Dover Publications, Inc.
31 East 2nd Street
Mineola, N.Y. 11501

Note

If you like animals, here are 49 puzzles and activities featuring your favorite zoo friends: follow-the-dots, mazes, search-a-word puzzles and many more. You'll see elephants, tigers, camels and others, all waiting for you to solve the puzzle and color in the pictures. Solutions begin on page 53.

Use the code to color in this glamorous peacock!

Look at these snakes carefully. Then cross out the one that is different from the rest.

Draw a line from each zoo animal to its shadow.

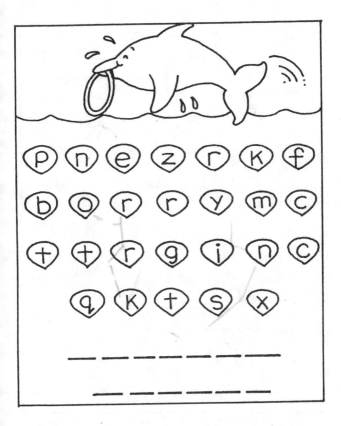

To find out what this dolphin likes to do, circle the first seashell and then every other one after that. Then fill in the blanks with the circled letters.

7

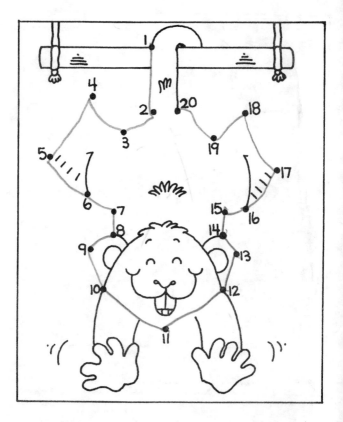

Look at me here, I can be quite a clown,
I'm using my tail to hang upside down.

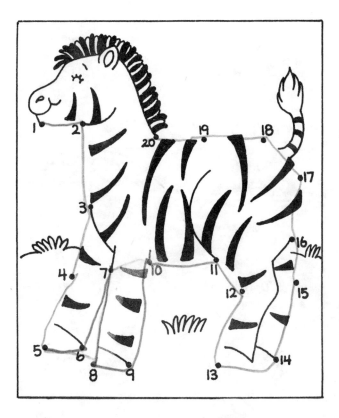

I've got black and white stripes from my hooves to my
    mane—
Without them I fear I'd look rather plain.

Have some fun and draw a line from each zoo animal on the left to the item it rhymes with on the right.

Unscramble the letters to find out what kind of bear Ivan is. Write the word in the spaces provided.

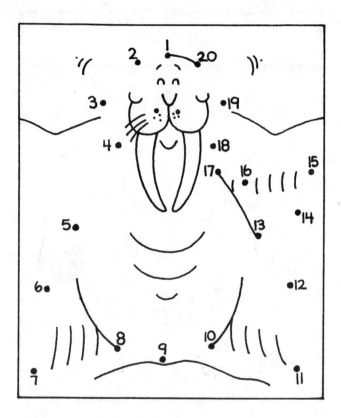

At first my long tusks might look out of place,
But they don't bother me—they're part of my face!

Can you find the twin of the turtle with the arrow?
When you do, draw a line to connect them together.

Draw a line from each animal to what it says.

Use the code to find out what animal is peeking out of the pool at us.

If you look at my back, you'll see a big bump.
It's where I store water and it's called a hump.

Put one letter in each empty box so that the words will describe the pictures.

Hippopotamus

sat
_____   _____

_____   _____

_____   _____

_____   _____

_____   _____

How many words can you spell using the letters in
"Hippopotamus"? One is already done for you.

18

1. It is big.
2. Its mouth is open.
3. Its eye is shut.

Use the clues to find out which fish is the head of its school.

m____se   ff

d____r   oo

bu____alo   ee

Choose the double letters at the right that will help to
spell the names of these three zoo animals.

An octopus has ___ arms.

A rhinoceros has 1 or
___ horns.

A crocodile has ___
legs.

4   8   2

Choose the correct number from below to fill in each
blank.

This lion needs 12 pieces of meat to feed his family.
Circle the box with the correct amount in it.

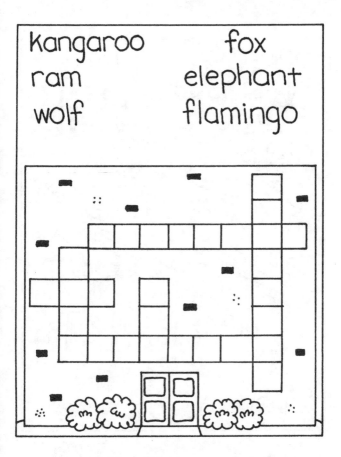

kangaroo   fox
ram   elephant
wolf   flamingo

Write the words above onto the zoo building below in such a way that all the letters are in the right place.

23

This zoo has a talking parrot! Count how many times
he has said "Hello" and write that number in the circle.

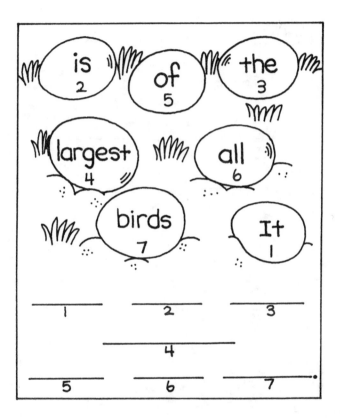

Write the words from the ostrich eggs onto the blanks in the order of their numbers. This will tell you something interesting about the ostrich.

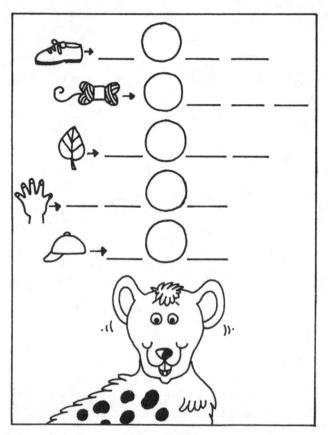

Find out the name of this animal by writing in the name of each picture. The circled letters will reveal the answer.

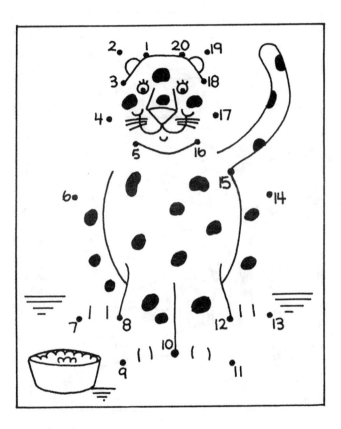

Start right away and connect all the dots;
I'm a very big cat who's covered with spots.

There are five lizards hidden in the zoo's pond. Can you find and circle them?

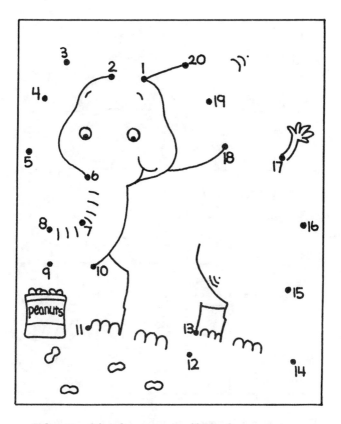

I'd eat nothing but peanuts if I had my way.
When you see who I am, color me gray.

large
hot
rain
vines
damp

b	d	v	z	l
r	a	i	n	a
u	m	n	h	r
y	p	e	o	g
k	c	s	t	e

This toucan was brought from the rain forest to live at the zoo. The words below describe the forest. Try to find them in the box and circle them.

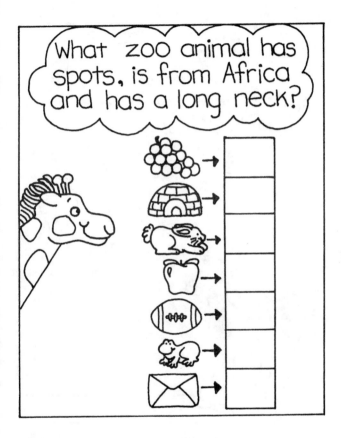

To find out the answer to the question below, write the first letter of the word each picture represents in the empty box beside it.

b c u

_ _ _

w n f a

_ _ _ _

o y p n

_ _ _ _

Unscramble the letters to find out what we call each of these baby or small animals.

Draw a line from each animal to its missing tail.

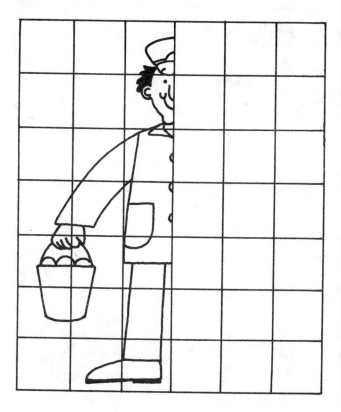

The animals at the zoo are hungry, and you can help them! Finish drawing the other half of the zoo keeper so he can feed them.

Sean has bought a cup of fish. Fill in all the blanks with the letter "e" to find out what the seal is saying to him.

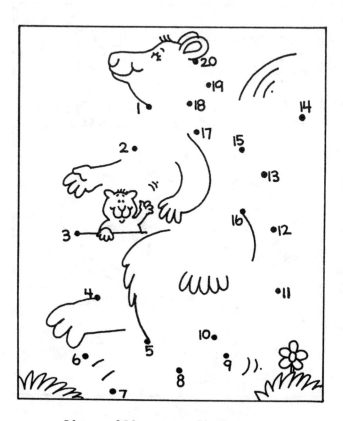

I hop and I hop, up and back down—
This is the way I move through town!

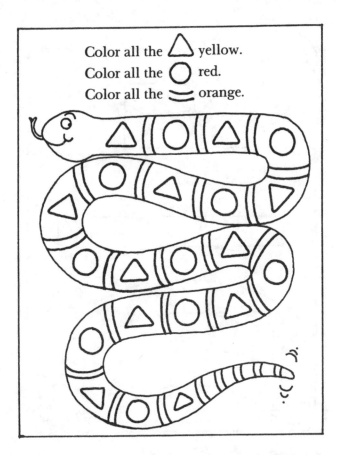

Color all the △ yellow.
Color all the ○ red.
Color all the ≋ orange.

Follow the directions to color the pattern on this snake.

37

Oh-oh! One of Mrs. Cougar's cubs is lost. Help him find his way back!

Circle all the things that rhyme with "bat."

The zoo is home to many different kinds of birds. Look at the picture clues below and use them to fill in the crossword puzzle.

Look at the three steps that show you how to draw a porcupine. Then try to draw one in the blank space on this page.

Follow the line from each animal to its cage.

abcdef
ghijkl
mnopqr
stuvwx
yz

l ☐
d ☐
c ☐
h ☐
b ☐
h ☐
m ☐
d ☐

In each empty box, write in the letter that comes after the one beside it. (Use the complete alphabet to help.) When you're done, you'll find out what this zoo doctor sometimes gives a sick animal.

43

Here are two snapshots of a koala. Draw three things in the top one so that it matches the bottom one exactly.

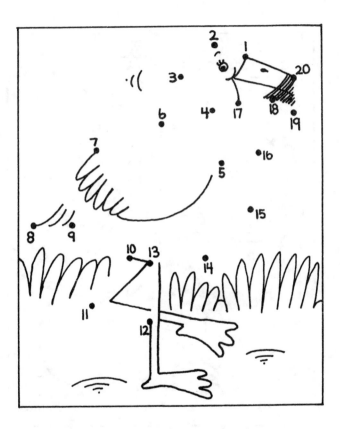

Most birds stand on two legs, I often stand on one;
I really do not mind it, I think it's kind of fun.

Something's not right at the zoo! Look at the picture and find five things that are wrong.

Look carefully at the two pictures of the panda. In the top picture, circle the three things that make it different from the bottom picture.

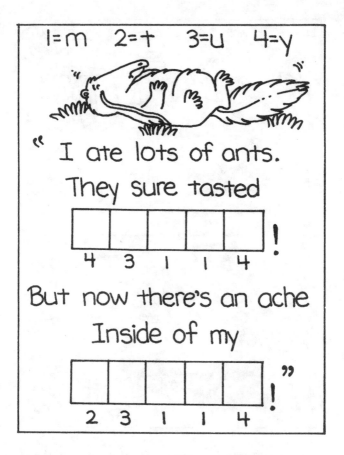

1=m 2=t 3=u 4=y

" I ate lots of ants.
They sure tasted

4	3	1	1	4

!

But now there's an ache
Inside of my

2	3	1	1	4

! "

Use the number code to find out what this anteater is saying.

48

Each monkey has a brother who is in exactly the same pose. Connect the matching pairs with a line.

See which prairie dog will find his way out of the
burrow to the earth's surface at the top of the picture.
(One of them has no path to the top.)

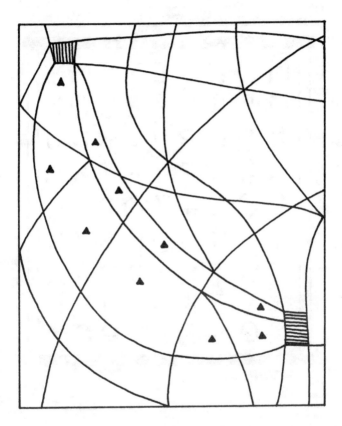

The zoo keeper is going to give the gorilla a snack. To find out what it is, color all the spots with a ▲ yellow.

```
M O N K E Y L M Y
O B C Q K E G O K
N D H R V K K N U
K C A F Y N T K M
E Q E J Z O D E O
Y E K N O M B Y N
T W P X I B S A K
Z Y E K N O M L E
M O N K E Y P C Y
```

The monkeys are always fun to watch! Can you find the word "monkey" eight times in the cage? Look up, down, forward and backward.

Solutions

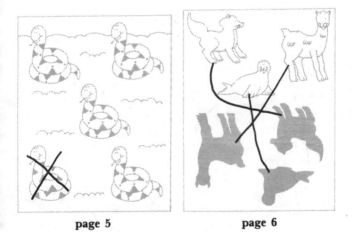

page 5

page 6

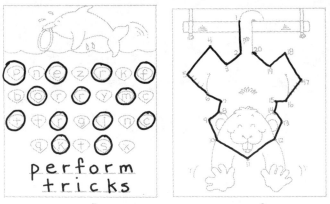

page 7

page 8

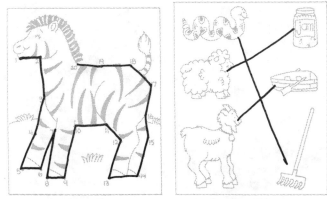

page 9

page 10

page 11

page 12

page 13

page 14

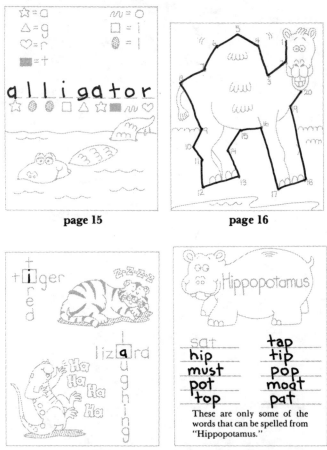

☆ = a   ∽ = o
△ = g   □ = i
♡ = r   ▯ = l
■ = t

a l l i g a t o r
☆ ▯ ▯ □ △ ☆ ■ ∽ ♡

page 15

page 16

t**i**ger   z-z-z-z
ired

liz**a**rd
a
u
g
h
i
n
g
Ha Ha Ha Ha Ha

page 17

Hippopotamus

sat   tap
hip   tip
must   pop
pot   moat
top   pat

These are only some of the
words that can be spelled from
"Hippopotamus."

page 18

56

page 19

page 20

m**oo**se   ff

d**ee**r   oo

bu**ff**alo   ee

page 21

An octopus has **8** arms.

A rhinoceros has 1 or
2 horns.

A crocodile has **4**
legs.

page 22

57

kangaroo   fox
ram   elephant
wolf   flamingo

```
              K
              a
   elephant   n
 w        r   g
 f o x    a   a
 l        r   r
 f l a m i n g o
              o
```

page 23

Hello Hello
Hello Hello
Hello
Hello Hello
Hello
Hello Hello
Hello
12

page 24

is of the
largest all
birds It

It is the
largest
of all birds

page 25

s h o e
y a r n
l e a f
h a n d
c a p

page 26

58

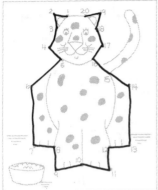

page 27

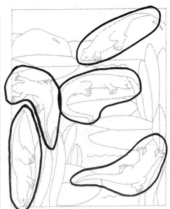

page 28

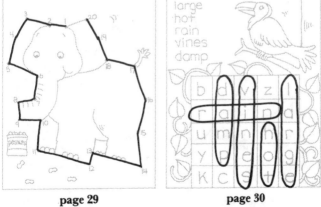

page 29

large
hot
rain
vines
damp

page 30

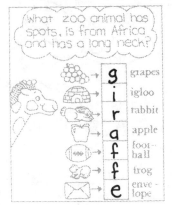

page 31

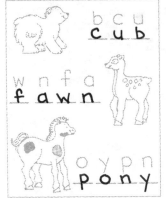

page 32

page 33

page 35

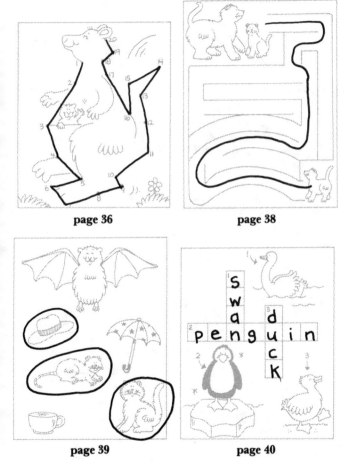

page 36

page 38

page 39

page 40

page 42

page 43

page 44

page 45

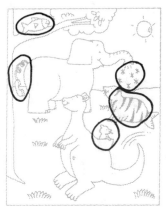

page 46

page 47

1=m 2=t 3=u 4=y

" I ate lots of ants.
They sure tasted

| Y | U | M | M | Y | !
  4   3   1   1

But now there's an ache
Inside of my

| T | U | M | M | Y | ! "
  2   3   1   1   4

page 48

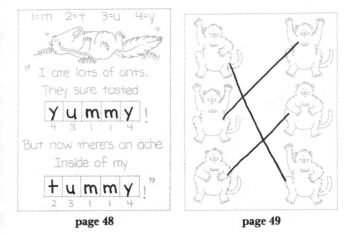

page 49

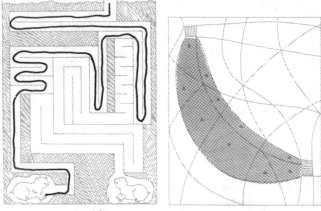

page 50

page 51

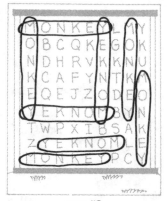

page 52